The New Novello Choral Edition

JOHANNES BRAHMS

A German Requiem

Ein deutsches Requiem

Op.45

for soprano and baritone soloists, SATB and orchestra

Revised with a new English translation by Michael Pilkington

Order No: NOV 072492

NOVELLO PUBLISHING LIMITED

It is requested that on all concert notices and programmes acknowledgement is made to 'The New Novello Choral Edition'.
Es wird gebeten, auf sämtlichen Konzertankündigungen und Programmen 'The New Novello Choral Edition' als Quelle zu erwähnen.
Il est exigé que toutes les notices et programmes de concerts, comportent des remerciements à 'The New Novello Choral Edition'.

Cover illustration: first page of the first edition of Brahms's *Ein deutsches Requiem*, published by Rieter-Biedermann in 1868.

Published in Great Britain by Novello Publishing Limited
Head Office: 14/15 Berners Street, LONDON, W1T 3LJ

Sales and Hire: Music Sales Distribution Centre,
Newmarket Road, Bury St Edmunds, Suffolk IP33 3YB
Tel +44 (0)1284 702600   Fax +44 (0)1284 768301

Web: www.musicsales.com   e-mail: music@musicsales.co.uk

All Rights reserved   Printed in Great Britain

Excerpt from the Preface to the 1947 edition

Brahms's *Ein deutsches Requiem* (Op.45) is held by some to have been written in memory of Schumann, by others in memory of the composer's mother. There is no need to decide for either theory to the total exclusion of the other, for men's minds may work to the one end under as many stimuli in art as they do in life. Max Kalbeck informs us that the chorus 'Denn alles Fleisch, es ist wie Gras' was originally planned as the second movement (a slow, saraband-like scherzo) of an early sonata for two pianofortes, which was afterwards re-cast as the D minor Pianoforte Concerto. Kalbeck holds that this concerto (Op.15) was intended to be a memorial to Schumann, whose madness and tragic death had so deeply affected the youthful Brahms; but that not being satisfied with it he 'erected two other monuments to the memory of Schumann, more noble in feeling and more perfect in their art,' in the C minor Symphony and *Ein deutsches Requiem.* This view of the case may well be right; we know that the thoughtful young Brahms was so obsessed by the fate of his friend and mentor that when he heard Beethoven's ninth symphony for the first time, in 1856, the first movement of it seemed to speak to him directly of the Schumann tragedy. On the other hand, Madame Schumann thought that the Requiem was written in memory of Brahms's mother, although Brahms had never expressly said so; and this was the view taken by the composer's lifelong friend, Joachim, at a memorial festival at Meiningen, in 1899. The mother had died inn 1865. The Requiem seems to have been begun in 1866, and to have been finished – all but the fifth number, which was an afterthought – in 1867. No. 5 – the aria 'Ihr habt nun Traurigkeit' – was written at Bonn in May, 1868, and we have Brahms's own testimony that this movement at any rate was prompted by the memory of his mother.

The first three movements of the work were given in Vienna on December 1, 1867, under Herbeck. It had a mixed reception. The first two movements received some applause, but the third movement was greeted with many expressions of disapproval; the continual pedal point – intensified, it is said, by the too vigorous work of the drummer – had a disagreeable effect on the audience. On Good Friday (April 10, 1868), the whole of the Requiem (except No.5) was given in the cathedral at Bremen, under Reinthaler, the baritone solos being sung by Otto Schelper (not Stockhausen, as is commonly stated); it was repeated on the 27th of the same month - not in the cathedral this time, but at the 'Union'. In the following weeks the soprano aria was added, and the complete Requiem was given at the Leipzig Gewandhaus on February 18, 1869, under Reinecke. Numerous performances followed quickly in other German towns. It was given in English at a private meeting in Sir Henry Thompson's house in London on July 7, 1871, the orchestral part being played as a pianoforte duet by Lady Thompson and Cipriani Potter. The Requiem was also produced about this time at a students' concert of the Royal Academy of Music; but the first public performance of which we have any record is that at a Philharmonic Society's concert in St. James's Hall on April 2, 1873, under Mr. Cusins, the solos being taken by Miss Sophie Ferrari and Mr. Santley.

Ein deutsches Requiem, as will be seen at once, has nothing in common with the ordinary Requiem Mass; verbal purists have even disputed its claim to be called a Requiem at all, since it offers up no prayer for the dead. The text is freely selected from the Bible and the Apocrypha; the several sources of it may be indicated here:

1st Movement:	Matthew v.,4; Psalm cxxvi., 5, 6
2nd Movement:	I. Peter i., 24, 25; James v., 7, 8; Isaiah xxxv., 10
3rd Movement:	Psalm xxxix., 4-7; Wisdom iii., 1
4th Movement:	Psalm lxxxiv., 1, 2, 4
5th Movement:	John xvi., 22; Ecclesiasticus li., 27; Isaiah lxvi., 13
6th Movement:	Hebrews xiii., 14; I Corinthians xv., 5-52, 54-55; Revelation iv., 11
7th Movement:	Revelation xiv., 13

That Brahms was both an earnest thinker and an assiduous student of the Bible is evident, though it would not be wise to try to fix the exact measure of his orthodoxy. We are told by Kalbeck that 'nothing made him angrier than to be taken for an orthodox church composer on account of his sacred compositions'. Probably he was always more philosopher than theologian. When sending Herzogenberg the 'Vier Ernste Gesänge' (Op.121) in June, 1896, he jokingly anticipated censure for his 'unchristian principles,' the texts, as Kalbeck says, being in part 'not only anti-dogmatic but irreligious' (*ungläubig*). Brahms's freedom from purely theological prepossessions may be seen in his correspondence with Reinthaler over the Requiem. Reinthaler, who was the organist at Bremen Cathedral, urged him to make the work more definitely orthodox. 'It occupies,' he says in a letter of October 5, 1867, 'not only religious but purely Christian ground. The second number deals with the prediction of the return of the Lord, and in the last number but one there is express reference to the mystery of the resurrection of the dead, 'Siehe, ich sage euch ein Geheimnis'. For the Christian mind, however, there is lacking the point on which everything turns, namely the redeeming death of Jesus. Perhaps the passage 'Tod, wo ist dein Stachel?' would be the best point at which to introduce this idea, either briefly in the movement itself, before the fugue, or in a new movement. Moreover you say in the last movement 'Selig sind die Toten, die in dem Herren sterben, von num an' ('Blessed are the dead which in the Lord are sleeping from henceforth'), that is to say, after Christ has finished the work of redemption.' Brahms's reply is that he is writing for humanity as a whole, and has deliberately passed over verses like that of John iii., 16[1], while he has selected others 'because I am a musician, because I needed them, because I cannot dispute the "from henceforth" of my revered poets, or strike it out,' which, reading between the lines, seems to mean simply that the Requiem is intended to be a human document rather than a theological argument. The text voices the perennial fluctuations of the human spirit between fear and hope, and its longing for consolation. The work has been accused of lack of unity, and in one sense, perhaps, rightly. Dramatic or fictive unity - which is the kind the critics of the Requiem have in view - is not easily attained in composite works of this kind; it might be possible to rearrange the grouping of one or two of the numbers without doing serious damage to the work. Nor is the ending above criticism. The chorus 'Herr, du bist würdig zu nehmen Preis und Ehre und Kraft', is so powerful that one at first feels that the real climax to have come here, and that the final chorus has only been added because of the impossibility of ending a Requiem in a mood of jubilation. But the point is hardly worth worrying over; and certainly not only does the work end poetically in the only way we could possibly feel to be the right one, but it is exquisitely and touchingly rounded off by a return to the thematic material of the opening chorus. Musically, at any rate, the unity of the Requiem is beyond dispute.

Ernest Newman

NOTES
Newman does not give references for his sources.
1   'For God so loved the world that he gave his only Son, that whoever believes in him should not perish but have eternal life.'

PREFACE

The music text of this new Novello score follows the full score of the Breitkopf & Härtel Complete Works edition, edited by Brahms's friend Eusebius Mandyczewski. Mandyczewski's sources were the autograph, Brahms's copy of the first edition, and the parts used for the first Viennese performance, conducted by the composer. The piano reduction has been modified in a few places from the Novello vocal score that this new edition supercedes to reflect more closely the orchestral score. Where both German and Italian tempo marks are given, the German is by Brahms and the Italian supplied by earlier English editors. Metronome marks, which were originally included by the composer, but later withdrawn, are included here for guidance.

The Translation

'It is a sure sign of an imperfect musical civilisation when a public that does
not know a foreign language prefers to hear foreign vocal works in the original.'
Donald Tovey[1]

This New Novello Choral Edition provides the text in both English and German. This will enable choral conductors to decide which language is the more appropriate to use in the particular circumstances of their own performance. It is hoped that this new translation will make performance in English in English-speaking countries a viable option.

'No translation could possibly substitute for [the original words of the Lutheran version of Scripture] at once the accepted English reading, the same number of syllables, words of the same or analogous meaning to identical notes, similar vowels to express the same feelings, and punctuation that admitted of breathing points at the same periods of phrases.'[2] The translator must decide on priorities in the attempt to provide a singable English version. Here they have been: to fit Brahms's rhythms as closely as possible; to give the English equivalent of the *meaning* of the German; to allow breathing points at the same places as the original; and to ensure singable vowels on high notes. When possible important words retain their position, but the natural German word order being very different from that of English this is not always possible without unreasonable distortion of the English language.

Finally, before starting the work, a decision must be taken as to the *style* of the language to use. A translation should at least attempt to match the style of the original text. To those who would argue that present day language should be used rather than an out-dated style I would point out that the result would soon become out-dated itself. Brahms used the text of the Lutheran Bible. Luther's translation from Hebrew (Old Testament) and Greek (New Testament) was made between 1523 and 1530. This has received various revisions over the years; the text given at the beginning of this vocal score is from the edition of 1855, available to Brahms at the time of the work's composition. The composer made further modifications of his own, which explains the occasional discrepancies between the text as laid out at the beginning, and that given below the music.

Previous English version have taken the King James Bible of 1611 as the equivalent and tried to fit this to Brahms's music, adjusting rhythms as necessary. Between 1526 and 1535 William Tyndale translated the New Testament and much of the Old Testament; There were no less than five further translations before that of 1611, all of them (including the King James) making considerable use of Tyndale, though without acknowledgement. These have all been used in the preparation of this edition, as have more modern translations, from the Revised of 1881 to the Revised English of 1989.

Rather than altering Brahms's rhythms to fit the English, the English has been matched, as far as possible, to the rhythms of the music. In some passages Luther's understanding of the original Hebrew was not the same as that of the English translators. In such a situation it is clearly better to translate the German directly, giving the meaning as the composer understood it, rather than using the English version of the same text, with its different interpretation. Specific problems are discussed below.

II, bb.82-3. 90: many translations of the Requiem have 'Christ' for 'Lord'; though this fits the music better it is misleading, in that no bible translation uses the word 'Christ' in this sentence.

II, bb.109-119: the English here is specifically designed to match the hemiolas in the music. Almost all English bibles refer to 'the early and the latter rain', modified in the twentieth century to 'the early and late rains'; the Jerusalem Bible has 'the autumn rains and the spring rains'. The German of 1855 clearly has the morning rain and the evening rain, 'den Morgenregen und Abendregen'. Interestingly, by 1892 this has been changed to 'den Frühregen und Spätregen'.

II, b.244: though King James and most subsequent translations have 'flee away' the older translations have 'vanish away', which is closer to the German text.

III, bb.1-16: the German has nothing of the King James words about 'frailty'.

III, bb.105-114: the word setting of the first two phrases is not ideal, but nor is it in the German. The meaning of the German in the third phrase is quite different from that given in most English bibles.

III, bb.173-5: this verse from *The Wisdom of Solomon* begins with 'Aber' in Luther and 'But' in King James. Brahms omits 'Aber', and with the change of context 'For' seemed more suitable than 'But'. It is with regret that I have not used Tyndale's translation - 'the pain of death shall not touch them', but the music did not allow it.

IV, bb.3-13: the familiar Prayer Book words are wonderful, but for speaking, not singing - 'O how amiable are thy dwellings.'

V, bb.18-26: the two earliest English versions read - 'For like as a child is comforted of his mother, so I shall comfort you.'

VI, bb.82-104, 127-150: Brahms uses the same music for two different sentences, adjusting rhythms to suit; it therefore seems allowable to do the same in English, though making the adjustments at different points.

VI, b.154: In this bar *only* Brahms has 'Stachel!' rather than 'Stachel?'

VI, b.159: 'Two words are translated in the New Testament by "hell", namely "Hades" and "Gehenna".' "Hades" is the Latin translation of "Sheol", and means literally "the unseen world", or "the grave". "Gehenna" is, however, the word most often used for future punishment.'[3] "Sheol" is the word used in this passage from Corinthians.

VI, b.214: To avoid repetition Brahms altered the first of Luther's two uses of 'geschaffen' to 'erschaffen'. though both may be translated 'created'.

VI, b.216-218 (alto): 'for thy will's sake' is the expression used in nearly all the early translations, only altered to 'for thy pleasure' in 1611.

VI, bb.297, 323: Alto note 1: 'g' in all sources; the octaves with the bass and the bare choral setting on the strong part of the measure allow one to assume this is a slip of the pen.' Mandyczewski

VII, b.3: there appears to be no solution to the problem of the German for 'dead' having two syllables and therefore two notes. In later passages the repetition of 'blessed' has been used to ease the difficulty.

I must record my thanks to members of the East Surrey Choral Society and to Ameral Gunson for their assistance and advice on the translation. This advice, though gratefully received, was not always accepted, and any faults are my own. I must also thank Norman Taylor for his lengthy loan of an 1855 copy of the Lutheran Bible.

Michael Pilkington
Old Coulsdon
April 1999

1   D.F. Tovey, *Essays in Musical Analysis*, Introduction to Volume V (1937).
2   George Macfarren, Preface to the Novello edition of Bach's *Christmas Oratorio*.
3   Rev. C.H. Wright (ed.), *Bible Reader's Encyclopaedia and Concordance* (1962).

A GERMAN REQUIEM

Ein deutsches Requiem

German/English

I

Selig sind, die da Leid tragen, denn sie sollen
getröstet werden.

Matthäus 5:4

Die mit Tränen säen, werden mit Freuden
ernten.
Sie gehen hin und weinen, und tragen edlen
Samen, und kommen mit Freuden und
bringen ihre Garben.

Psalm 126: 5-6

II

Denn alles Fleisch es ist wie Gras, und alle
Herrlichkeit der Menschen wie des Grases
Blume. Das Gras ist verdorret, und die Blume
abgefallen.

1 Petrus 1:24

So seid nun geduldig, liebe Brüder, bis auf die
Zukunft des Herrn. Siehe, ein Ackermann
wartet auf die köstliche Frucht der Erde, und
ist geduldig darüber, bis er empfange den
Morgenregen und Abendregen.

Jakobus 5:7

Aber des Herrn Wort bleibet in Ewigkeit.

1 Petrus 1:25

Die Erlöseten des Herrn werden wieder kommen,
und gen Zion kommen mit Jauchzen; ewige
Freude wird über ihrem Haupte sein; Freude
und Wonne werden sie ergreifen und Schmerz
und Seufzen wird weg müssen.

Jesaja 35:10

III

Herr, lehre doch mich, daß es ein Ende mit mir
haben muß, und mein Leben ein Ziel hat, und
ich davon muß.
Siehe, meine Tage sind einer Hand breit bei dir,
und mein Leben ist wie nichts vor dir. Wie
gar nichts sind alle Menschen, die doch so
sicher leben!
Sie gehen daher wie Schemen, und machen sich
viel vergebliche Unruhe; sie sammlen und
wissen nicht wer es kriegen wird.
Nun, Herr, weß soll ich mich trösten? Ich hoffe
auf dich.

Psalm 39:5-8

Der Gerechten Seelen sind in Gottes Hand, und
keine Qual rühret sie an.

Weisheit 3:1

I

Blest are they that sorrow bear, for to them shall
be given comfort.

Matthew 5:4

They that sow lamenting shall reap a joyful
harvest.
Who goeth forth with weeping, and beareth
precious seed for sowing, shall come home
rejoicing and bring his good sheaves with him.

Psalm 126: 5-6

II

Behold all flesh is as the grass, and all the
goodliness of man is as the flower that fadeth.
The grass is now withered and the flower
thereof is fallen.

1 Peter 1:24

Now therefore be patient, my dear brethren, unto
the coming of the Lord. See how the
husbandman waiteth for the earth's precious
fruit to ripen, and long he waiteth with
patience, until the coming of morning rainfall
and evening showers.

James 5:7

But yet the Lord's word standeth for evermore.

1 Peter 1:25

And the ransomed of the Lord shall return with
singing, unto Zion coming rejoicing.
Unending gladness forever on their heads shall
be. Pleasure and gladness ever shall possess
them, and grief and sorrow, they shall vanish.

Isaiah 35:10

III

Lord, make me to know that the measure of my
days is set; that my life hath an ending, and I
must go hence.
Surely, all my days here are but a span long to
thee, and my whole life is as naught to thee.
Ah, as nothing every man living, he trusts
himself but vainly.
He walketh about as a shadow; he is disquieted
and is greatly troubled in spirit; his riches, he
knoweth not who shall gather them.
Now Lord, wherein is my comfort? My hope is in
thee.

Psalm 39:4-7

For the righteous souls are in the hand of God,
and no more pain touches them now.

Wisdom of Solomon 3:1

IV

Wie lieblich sind deine Wohnungen, Herr
  Zebaoth!
Meine Seele verlanget und sehnet sich nach den
  Vorhöfen des Herrn; mein Leib und Seele
  freuen sich in dem lebendigen Gott.

Psalm 84: 2, 3

Wohl denen, die in deinem Hause wohnen; die
  loben dich immerdar.

Psalm 84: 5

V

Ihr habt auch nun Traurigkeit; aber ich will euch
  wieder sehen, und euer Herz soll sich freuen,
  und eure Freude soll niemand von euch
  nehmen.

Johannes 16: 22

Sehet mich an: ich habe eine kleine Zeit Mühe
  und Arbeit gehabt und habe grossen Trost
  funden.

Jesus Sirach 51: 35

Ich will euch trösten, wie einen seine Mutter
  tröstet.

Jesaja 66: 13

VI

Denn wir haben hier keine bleibende Stadt,
  sondern die zukünftige suchen wir.

Hebräer 13: 14

Siehe, ich sage euch ein Geheimnis: Wir werden
  nicht alle entschlafen, wir werden aber alle
  verwandelt werden.
Und dasselbe plötzlich in einem Augenblick, zu
  der Zeit der letzten Posaune. Denn es wird
  die Posaune schallen, und die Toten werden
  auferstehen unverweslich, und wir werden
  verwandelt werden.

1. Korinther 15: 51, 52

Dann wird erfüllet werden das Wort, das
  geschrieben stehet:
Der Tod ist verschlungen in den Sieg.
Tod, wo ist dein Stachel? Hölle, wo ist dein Sieg?

1. Korinther 15: 54, 55

Herr, du bist würdig zu nehmen Preis und Ehre,
  und Kraft; denn du hast all Dinge geschaffen,
  und durch deinen Willen haben sie das
  Wesen, und sind geschaffen.

Offenbarung 4: 11

VII

Selig sind die Todten, die in dem Herrn sterben,
  von nun an. Ja der Geist spricht, daß sie
  ruhen von ihrer Arbeit, denn ihre Werke
  folgen ihnen nach.

Offenbarung 14: 13

IV

How lovely are all thy dwellings fair, O Lord of
  hosts!
For my soul now is yearning and longing sore for
  the blest courts of the Lord; my heart and
  flesh cry out for joy unto the living God.

Psalm 84: 1-2

How blest are they that in thy house are dwelling;
  they give thee praise evermore.

Psalm 84: 4

V

Ye now are sorrowful, but yet I will again behold
  you and then your hearts shall be joyful, and
  this your joyfulness no man taketh from you.

John 16: 22

Now behold me: I had but for a little while labour
  and trouble to bear, and yet great comfort now
  I have found.

Ecclesiasticus 51: 27

For I will comfort, like as a mother giveth
  comfort.

Isaiah 66: 13

VI

Here on earth have we no continuing home,
  rather we seek one to come.

Hebrews 13: 14

Lo, I will show unto you a mystery: we shall not
  all slumber, but we shall all be changed,
in a moment, the twinkling of an eye, at the
  sounding of the last trumpet. Then the
  trumpet shall be sounded, and the dead shall
  all be raised up incorruptible, and we shall all
  be changed.

1 Corinthians 15: 51-52

Then shall be fulfilled the word that is written
  thus: Now death is swallowed up in victory;
Death, where is thy victory? Hades, where is thy
  sting?

1 Corinthians 15: 54-55

Lord thou art worthy to gather praise and honour
  and power, for it is thou hast all things
  created, and for thy will's sake they are and
  have their being, and were created.

Revelation 4: 11

VII

Blessed are the dead, which in the Lord are
  sleeping from henceforth: Yea, saith the Spirit,
  they may rest now from all their labours; their
  works shall follow after them.

Revelation 14: 13

A GERMAN REQUIEM

Ein deutsches Requiem

I

4

6

14

II

* see Preface

15

18

* see Preface

* see Preface

24

28

30

* see Preface

32

40

III

* see Preface

42

* Bass note 1: d, Complete Works

44

* see Preface

49

50

52

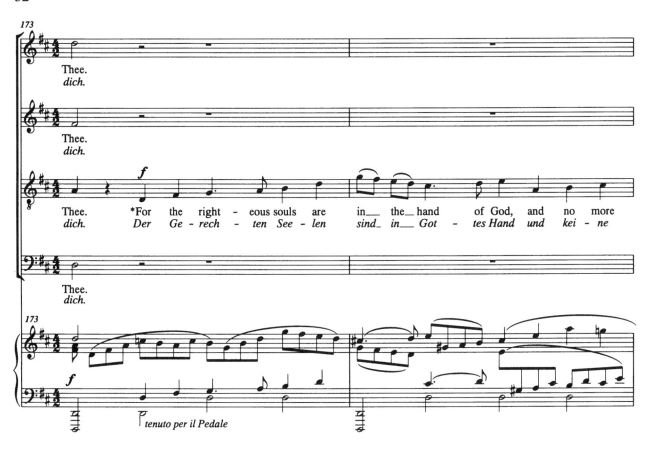

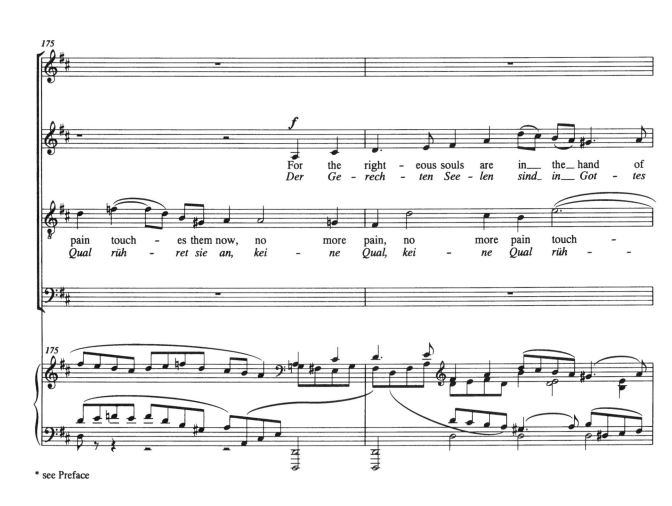

* see Preface

53

55

58

60

63

64

70

V

76

* see Preface

82

VI

* see Preface

89

* see Preface

* see Preface

95

96

98

* see Preface

100

106

* g' in sources, see Preface.

* g' in sources, see Preface.

113

VII

sleep - - - ing from hence - - - forth.
ster - - - ben von nun_____ an.

122

126

Published by Novello Publishing Limited
Music setting by Stave Origination

Printed and bound in Great Britain by Caligraving Limited